Treat Your Own Achilles Tendinitis

by
Jim Johnson, PT

This book was designed to provide accurate information in regard to the subject matter covered. It is sold with the understanding that the author is not engaged in rendering medical, psychological, or other professional services. If expert assistance is required, the services of a professional should be sought.

This edition published by
Dog Ear Publishing
4010 W. 86th Street, Ste H
Indianapolis, IN 46268

www.dogearpublishing.net

ISBN: 978-145751-092-2
Library of Congress Control Number:
This book is printed on acid-free paper.

Printed in the United States of America

How This Book Is Set Up

✓ **Learn how your Achilles tendon is put together in** *Chapter 1.*

✓ **Find out what can go wrong with the Achilles tendon in** *Chapter 2.*

✓ **Be aware of the typical course that Achilles tendon problems take in** *Chapter 3.*

✓ **Learn how you can treat your Achilles tendon problem in** *Chapter 4.*

✓ **Find out how much activity is safe to do while your Achilles tendon heals in** *Chapter 5.*

✓ **Monitor your progress with the tools in** *Chapter 6.*

Why Is The Print In This Book So Big?

People who read my books sometimes wonder why the print is so big in many of them. Some tend to think it's because I'm trying to make a little book bigger or a short book longer.

Actually, the main reason I use bigger print is for the same reason I intentionally write short books, usually under 100 pages–it's just plain easier to read and get the information quicker!

You see, the books I write address common, everyday problems that people of *all* ages have. In other words, the "typical" reader of my books could be a teenager, a busy housewife, a CEO, a construction worker, or a retired senior citizen with poor eyesight. Therefore, by writing books with larger print that are short and to the point, *everyone* can get the information quickly and with ease. After all, what good is a book full of useful information if nobody ever finishes it?

Table of Contents

The Problem Isn't What You Think It Is

The Achilles tendon is the largest and strongest tendon in the human body. Interestingly enough though, it's also one of the most troublesome. To understand its problems, you first have to know a little bit about its structure. So without wasting any time, let's just jump right in…

The Achilles Tendon Few People Know About

If I told you to glance down at your Achilles tendon, most people would probably look down at the back of their legs, and see something like this…

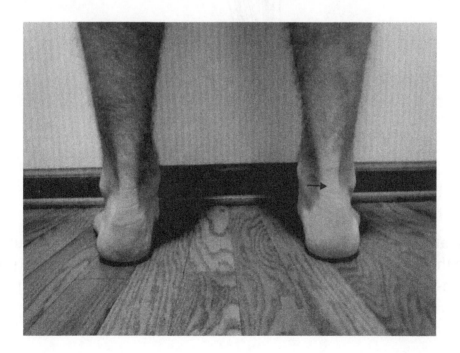

The Achilles tendon, which the lower arrow points to, looks like a thick, round cable or piece of rope – at least that's what it looks like *on the surface*. If we could peel away the skin and fat, and move down to the next layer, we would get a quite different view of things…

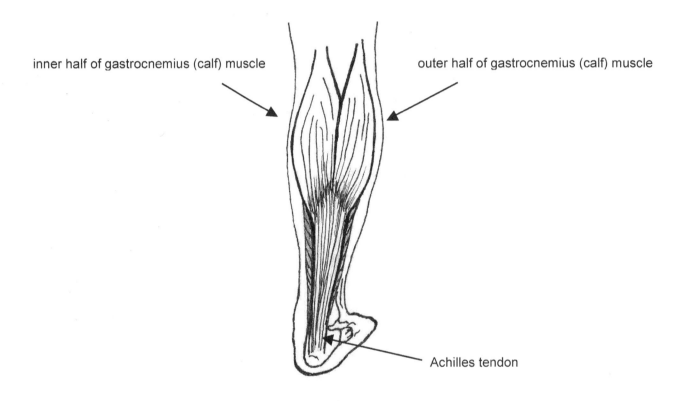

Figure 1. Looking at the back of the right leg – the gastrocnemius (calf) muscle.
Note it has a distinct left and right half.

Looking at the above picture, one can't help but notice the huge bulk of tissue right above the Achilles tendon. Known as the *gastrocnemius* muscle (pronounced gas-tro-neem-e-us), this muscle consists of two parts, an inner and outer half.

And just underneath the gastrocnemius, is another muscle known as the *soleus*. As the picture below reveals, it's a long, flat muscle…

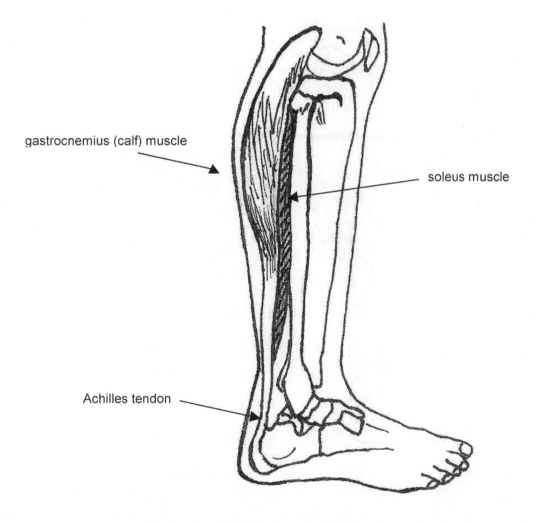

Figure 2. Looking at the right leg from the side.
Note that the soleus is buried deep to the gastrocnemius (calf) muscle.

However to get a really good look at the soleus muscle, we have to remove the gastrocnemius entirely, which gives us a more complete picture …

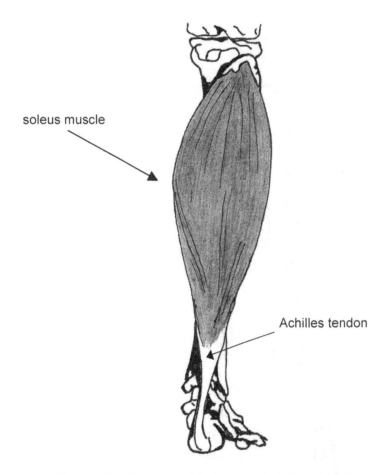

soleus muscle

Achilles tendon

Figure 3. Looking at the right leg from the back – the soleus muscle.

Wow! The soleus muscle doesn't seem quite as small as in the last picture, does it? While the gastrocnemius is bulky and sticks out, the soleus muscle is a pretty good size too, although it's much longer and flatter.

And together, the gastrocnemius and soleus muscles make up the bulk of your leg - and to a large degree – are responsible for it's shape, as this drawing reveals…

Figure 4. Looking at the left leg from the side.
Note how the gastrocnemius and soleus muscles make up the contour of the leg

Okay, we've spent a lot of time talking about the gastrocnemius and soleus muscles, but what do *they* have to do with the Achilles tendon? Well, as you've probably noticed by now, both of these muscles run up and down the leg, and connect to…..the Achilles tendon!

That's right, these muscles are very important to know about when you have trouble with your Achilles tendon, because they are linked *directly* to it.

And the following picture shows up close how things tie in…

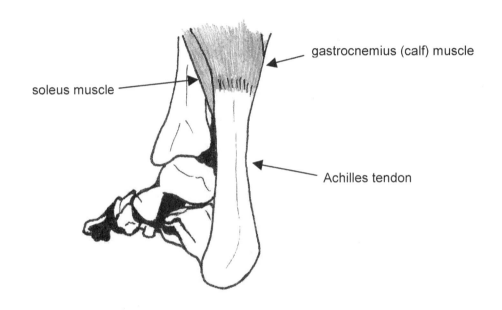

Figure 5. Looking at the foot from behind.
Note how the gastrocnemius and soleus muscles connect into the Achilles tendon.

What We See When We Look At the
Inside of the Achilles Tendon

Okay, so far we've learned that there are two big muscles in your leg that connect directly to the Achilles tendon. So that's all we need to know, right? Well, actually, that just scratches the surface. To fully solve an Achilles tendon problem, we've got to know the Achilles tendon inside and out. Since we know what the tendon looks like from the outside, let's take a closer look at its *internal* structure…

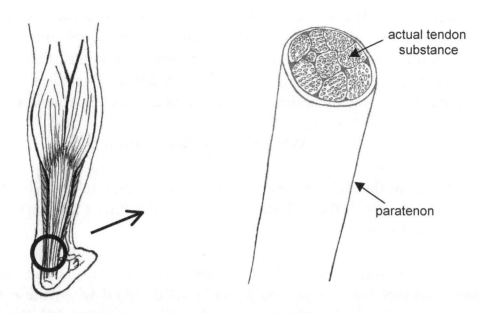

Figure 6. A close-up view of the internal structure of the Achilles tendon.

The above picture is a basic drawing of what a piece of the Achilles tendon looks like if you cut it straight across the top. As you can see, it's actually made up of a bunch of tiny little bundles, all encased in a sheath. *Very important to know, is that these bundles inside make up the actual tendon, while the "casing" that holds the tendon bundles together, is called the* **paratenon**. Here's a bird's eye view of the tendon, and it's sheath, the paratenon...

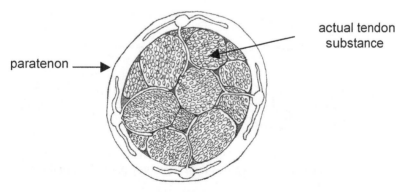

Figure 7. A cross sectional look at the Achilles tendon and its sheath. Note that the Achilles tendon itself is made up of many tiny bundles. A distinct, separate structure, called the paratenon, surrounds it.

Don't be fooled, while the Achilles tendon may seem like a simple rope-like structure at first glance, it's actually a little more complicated than that. You've got two muscles at one end, the gastocnemius and soleus, that blend together into the Achilles tendon, which is made up of many tiny bundles – all surrounded by the paratenon. And this raises an interesting question – what does it do?

What the Achilles Tendon Does

The job of the Achilles tendon is the same as all tendons – it connects muscle to bone. In the case of the Achilles, it connects the soleus and gastrocnemius muscles to your heel bone.

Keep in mind that all day long, you're contracting your soleus and gastrocnemius muscles as you move around. And when these two muscles are contracting, they're tightening up and pulling on your Achilles tendon – which makes your foot move in a motion called *plantarflexion*. Here's what your foot looks like when it *plantarflexes*…

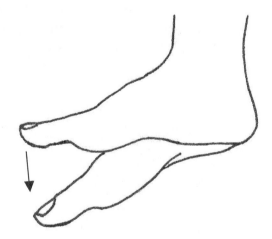

Figure 8. The motion of *plantar flexion*.
When one *plantarflexes* their foot, they push the foot down.

As you can see, the word plantarflexion is just a fancy medical name for the motion of pushing your foot *down*. Simple as that motion is, you're doing it all day long, *and* depending an awful lot on your Achilles tendon to help you do it!

The Most Common Problems People Have With Their Achilles Tendon

Now that you have a basic idea of how the Achilles tendon is put together and what it does, we can talk about what can go wrong with it. Probably the least severe problem you can have is a condition called *paratenonitis*. This is where the paratenon, the covering around the tendon, becomes inflamed.

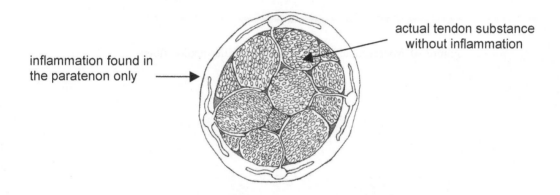

Figure 9. Paratenonitis is an inflammation of the paratenon.

The key here, is to know that in paratenonitis, researchers find inflammation in the paratenon *only*, while the actual tendon material itself is normal.

Next up is a condition called *tendinosis*. When you have Achilles tendinosis, the paratenon is just fine, but your problem is with the actual tendon itself. What kind of problem? Well, there's no inflammation to be found, but when researchers look at the tendon fibers under a microscope, they see that there is a big difference between the appearance of normal tendon fibers, and the way that tendon fibers look when one has tendinosis. We will take a more detailed look at this in the next chapter.

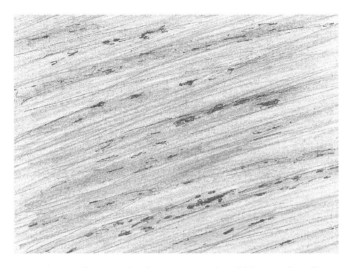

Figure 10. Microscopic view of normal Achilles tendon fibers.

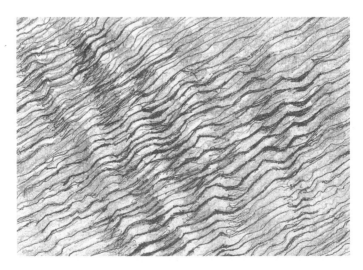

Figure 11. Microscopic view of what Achilles
tendon fibers look like when one has *tendinosis*.

Next up on the list of common Achilles tendon problems are tears. Tears (or ruptures) are generally classified as *partial* or *complete*. Here's a basic picture of each...

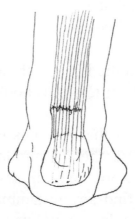

Figure 12. Looking at the foot from behind – a *partial* tear of the Achilles tendon.
Note that only part of the tendon is torn.

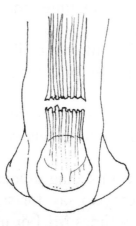

Figure 13 A *complete* tear of the Achilles tendon.
Note that the two ends are completely separated form one another.

So there you have it, the most common Achilles tendon problems people have. In a nutshell, they are…

- paratenonitis
- tendinosis
- partial tear
- complete tear

You'll note that what is *not* on the list is Achilles tendinitis. So what's up with that? I mean after all, that *is* in the title of this book.

Well, the truth of the matter, is that Achilles tendinitis is an incorrect term to describe *any* of the problems researchers commonly find in people with Achilles tendon pain. That's because the word "tendinitis" means inflammation of a tendon – and researchers simply don't find any inflammation in the tendons of patients who have pain in their Achilles tendon. Mind you, the paratenon may be inflamed, but not the actual tendon itself.

Unfortunately, the term "Achilles tendinitis" was coined a long time ago before most of the major research was done that showed a lack of inflammation in the tendon itself – but the term stuck over time, and is widely (but incorrectly) still used today. And that's the reason I chose to call this book "Treat Your Own Achilles Tendinitis" instead of something like, "Treat Your Own Achilles Paratenonitis". Who would go looking for that book?

But perhaps the bigger question is, you bought this book because you have pain in your Achilles tendon, so which one of the above problems do *you* have?

Well, figuring that out starts with seeing a doctor who will examine your foot and ankle. Even then, it's not easy to say for sure what the problem is just by physically looking at things. Many times MRI or ultrasound pictures are needed to get more information, and the real truth of the matter, is that a little piece of your Achilles tendon would have to be removed, and looked at under a microscope to be 100% positive that you have something like an inflamed paratenon.

However having said all that, There is a good reason as to why the rest of this book will probably help you. According to many research studies, the vast majority of people who have pain in their Achilles tendon, have *Achilles tendinosis*...

Study #1

- one study looked at 163 patients with chronic pain in their Achilles tendon (Astrom 1995)

- all had surgery

- pieces of the tendon were removed and later examined under a microscope

- 90% of patients were found to have *tendinosis*

Study #2

- this study looked at 27 patients with chronic pain in their Achilles tendon (Astrom 1996)

- all had surgery

- pieces of the tendon were removed and later examined under a microscope

- 21 of the 27 patients were found to have *tendinosis*

So as the research shows us, the majority of people who complain of pain in their Achilles tendon suffer from Achilles tendinosis – which is the very condition this book is intended to treat.

However, as always, it is recommended that you get a thorough exam and "okay" from your doctor before proceeding with the exercises in this book - just to make sure you don't have a serious medical condition. For example, we wouldn't want anyone with a torn Achilles tendon to be doing the exercises in the book, and a doctor can help sort out problems like these. For instance, one test doctors use to rule out a torn Achilles tendon is called the "calf squeeze test". It's been around since the late 1950's (Simmonds 1957) and goes like this…

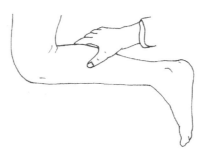

Figure 14. Starting position of the calf squeeze test – the foot is hanging freely.
Patient can be kneeling on a chair or lying flat on their stomach with the knee straight.

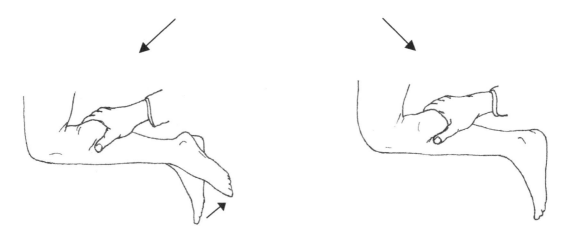

Figure 15. A negative test.
The calf is squeezed and the foot plantarflexes.
The Achilles tendon is likely not torn.

Figure 16. A positive test.
The calf is squeezed and the foot does ***not*** move (plantarflex).
A partial or complete tear of the Achilles tendon is likely.

Well, we've covered a lot of ground in this chapter, so here's a quick summary of the most important information you need to know about…

Key Points

✓ the *gastrocnemius* and *soleus* muscles come together and connect directly into the Achilles tendon

✓ a bunch of small bundles make up the Achilles tendon, which are encased in a sheath known as the *paratenon*

✓ the job of the Achilles tendon is to connect the gastrocnemius and soleus muscles to your heel bone.

✓ when the gastrocnemius and soleus muscles contract, they pull on the Achilles tendon, which makes your foot plantarflex, or push down

✓ the most common problem people have with their Achilles tendon is a condition called *tendinosis*, where there is no inflammation present, but rather a disorganization of the tendon fibers

What Went Wrong With Your Achilles Tendon

As you've learned in Chapter 1, when people have chronic (long-term) pain in their Achilles tendon, it's most of the time due to a condition called *tendinosis*. And we know this based on studies where chronic Achilles pain sufferers have ended up having surgery, a piece of their Achilles tendon was removed and examined under a microscope later, and *no* inflammation can be found in the tendon. While some readers may find this hard to believe, there has actually been a lot of studies showing that it's true, for instance…

Biopsy Studies Done on People with Achilles Tendon Pain

Study	# of samples	major histological findings reported
Shalabi 2002	15	-no inflammation found in tendon
Movin 1998	20	-no inflammation found in tendon
Movin 1997	40	-no inflammation found in tendon
Rolf 1997	58	-no inflammation found in tendon

But while there is normally no inflammation to be found in the tendons of people with long-term Achilles tendon pain, what researches *have found* are signs of **failed healing**, such as

- *disrupted and disorganized collagen fibers.* Collagen is a main ingredient that makes up your connective tissues – and it's having a hard time coming together properly in the tendon!

- *vascular proliferation (neovascularization).* Lots of blood vessels, arranged in irregular patterns, are found in the area – a sign that tendon healing is trying to take place!

Recall the pictures of microscopic tendon tissue that we saw in Chapter 1. Here is what normal Achilles tendon fibers should look like up close…

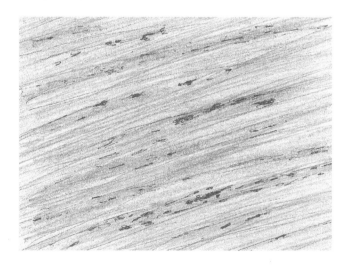

Figure 17. Microscopic view of normal tendon fibers.
Note the fibers are straight and organized.

Notice how straight and organized the tendon fibers are. That's the way things are *supposed* to be. Now check out the other drawing…

Figure 18. Microscopic view of what Achilles tendon fibers look like when one has tendinosis. Note the wavy, disorganized appearance of the fibers.

Wow, what a difference! And that's what your tendon looks like when you have Achilles tendinosis. Looks a little different from the first one, doesn't it? What a mess! As you can tell, there's *a lot* of disorganization going on there. Your body is trying to repair itself, but can't quite get its act together. But how did your Achilles tendon become so abnormal?

How Your Achilles Tendon Got Messed Up

The answer to the question, "How did your Achilles tendon become so abnormal?" can be answered in one word: *overuse*.

First, know that as you walk around throughout the day, you're contracting the gastrocnemius and soleus muscles, which are in turn pulling hard on your Achilles tendons (remember that tendons connect muscles to bones). And, just like most things in your body, your Achilles needs time (at some point) to rest and repair itself from this normal daily wear and tear.

Therefore, if you work your Achilles tendon, and give it *enough* time to recover each day, it's going to stay in good shape. We could then say that your Achilles tendon is "keeping up" with your activities. And all is well.

Now let's say you have a day where you've worked your Achilles tendon *more* than normal, or you're just using doing an activity you're simply not used to doing. For example, maybe you decided to run five miles one day rather than your usual two, or you were standing up on your toes a lot more than usual while painting. Well, of course this is going to cause *more* wear and tear on your Achilles than its normally used to, right?

Well, here's where the problems can start. **If** you give your Achilles tendon time to rest and recover (meaning that it has time to make the necessary repairs from this increased stress) *before* using it a lot again, your Achilles will be able to "keep up", stay in good working order, and will continue looking like this:

Figure 19. Normal tendon tissue that is able to "keep up" with what it's being asked to do.

On the other hand, if you *continue* to repeatedly work your Achilles harder than usual, it simply won't get enough time off to recover and make repairs. What will happen to it then? Well, *over time* your Achilles will be unable to "keep up" with the activities you are asking them to do, start to become internally disorganized, and will eventually end up looking like this:

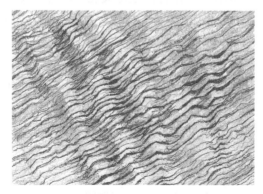

Figure 20. Abnormal tendon tissue that is *unable* to "keep up" with what it's being asked to do.

The moral of the story? The main problem in Achilles tendinosis is one of **failed tendon healing**. And the tendon has failed to heal because it was repeatedly put through stressful activities – and then not given enough repair time.

Two More Reasons Why
The Achilles Tendon Has Issues

I started this book out by saying that the Achilles tendon is the largest and strongest tendon in the human body. That being the case, you would think it would be able to take a lot of stress and be pretty resistant to problems.

Well, there are several big reasons why the Achilles has more than its fair share of problems compared to other tendons, and they all have to do with how it's put together. While we know from the first chapter that the gastrocnemius and soleus muscles run down the back of the leg and blend into the Achilles tendon, what I didn't tell you, was that the fibers of the Achilles actually *twist* as they head downward to the heel bone (Szaro 2009). Let me illustrate with a few pictures…

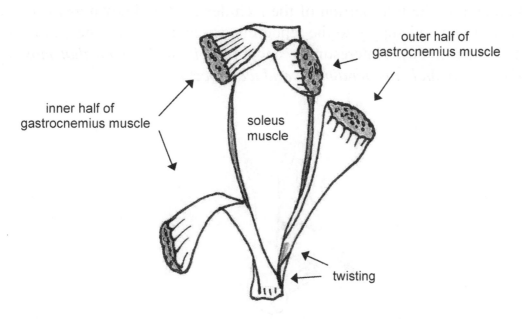

Figure 21. Looking at the right lower leg from the back.
The inner and out parts of the gastrocnemius have been cut revealing the soleus underneath.
Note the twisting of the fibers at the bottom where the Achilles tendon is.

Figure 22. Close-up view of the right Achilles tendon.
Note the twisting of the fibers at the bottom.

As you can see from the above picture, the fibers of the Achilles tendon don't run perfectly straight up and down, rather they start out straight, and then *twist*. Therefore, even though the Achilles looks like a piece of rope from the outside, it's actually a spiral structure! The point? Some researchers have theorized that this twisting of the fibers makes the Achilles more prone to wearing down and tearing.

The other reason that the Achilles has more than its share of problems? Well, it has to do with the blood supply to the tendon. Much research has revealed that there is an area in the mid-portion of the Achilles tendon, known as *the avascular zone*, where the blood supply to the tendon is extremely poor (Chen 2009, Zantop 2005, and Stein 2000). Interestingly enough, *it is at this spot that most people complain of pain, and most tendinosis and tears occur.*

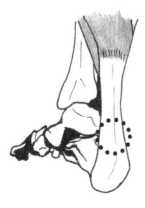

Figure 23. Looking at the back of the foot – the avascular zone.

Key Points

✓ **studies show that most people with Achilles tendon pain have tendinosis**

✓ **Achilles tendinosis does *not* involve inflammation**

✓ **rather, Achilles tendinosis is a condition of failed healing, which involves disorganized tendon fibers and an increase in blood vessels**

✓ **overusing the Achilles tendon without giving it enough time to rest, recover and repair itself is the main cause of tendinosis**

✓ **the twisting fibers of the Achilles tendon, as well as the poor blood supply to it's mid-portion most likely make it more prone to having problems**

3

What Will Happen To Your Achilles Tendon If You Do Nothing

If you have the flu and ask your doctor how long it will take you to get better, he or she will give you your *prognosis*. Prognosis can be defined as a prediction of the probable course and outcome of a disease. Practically speaking, it's your chances of recovery. So if you have Achilles tendinosis, what are your chances of getting back to normal if you did nothing?

Scientifically speaking, the only way to know for sure how long Achilles tendinosis will last if you just keep an eye on it, is to conduct what is called a *natural history study*. Natural history studies attempt to find out exactly how long a disease (or problem) will last on its own, naturally, without interference, by following a group of patients over time that have received little, or preferably no medical treatment. Let's have a look at the best one to date that's been done on Achilles tendinosis.

Taking the "Wait and See" Approach

Some of the best kind of natural history research you can look at to determine how long Achilles tendinosis lasts is what I call the "wait and see" studies. I call them this because in these studies, patients are randomly divided up into several groups, one of which is called a "wait and see" group.

If you're in this particular group, you get little or no treatment, which means you're basically just keeping an eye on your Achilles tendinosis so you can "wait and see" what it's going to do. On the next page is a summary of one such study.

- this study consisted of 75 patients with Achilles tendinosis (Rompe 2007)

- all had pain in the middle of their Achilles tendon for at least 6 months

- all patients had an ultrasound done, which revealed an irregular tendon structure

- patients were randomized to one of three groups. One group did specific exercises for the Achilles tendon, another group received shock-wave therapy to the Achilles tendon, and the last group took the "wait and see" approach.

- patients were followed-up 4 months later

- at that time, only 6 out of 25 patients that took the "wait and see" approach were either completely recovered or much improved

It's always good to check out these kinds of studies when one has a musculoskeletal problem, because many times pain problems *do* get better on their own – and if you have that knowledge, it can give you peace of mind, as well as save you a lot of time and money treating something that's going to get better over time anyway!

However in the case of Achilles tendinosis, we can see from the above study that taking the "wait and see" approach isn't a very effective way to manage your Achilles tendinosis if you've had it awhile – because only 24% of the people who took that route got better! So if you've been wondering if it'll get better on its own, well, the chances are good that it won't, and some kind of treatment is needed.

So the million dollar question is, if the majority of Achilles tendinosis sufferers fail to get better over time on their own, what treatments work best?

Well, that's exactly what the remainder of this book is all about: the best treatment you can do to get rid of your Achilles tendinosis in the shortest amount of time – *that you can do on your own.*

Key Points

✓ a prognosis is the prediction of the probable course and outcome of a disease

✓ "wait and see" studies tell us that the prognosis for most people who have had Achilles tendinosis longer than 6 months is poor if they don't get treatment

✓ only about 24% of patients may spontaneously recover

 A Surefire Way to Help Your Achilles Tendon *Finally* Heal

Probably the single most important piece of information to know when it comes to unlocking the mystery of getting rid of Achilles tendinosis, is realizing that the main problem is actually one of *failed tendon healing*. Therefore, it logically follows, that a successful treatment must be one that creates a healing environment for the Achilles tendon to finally repair itself. And this brings us to the main strategy of the treatment in this chapter – *improving the quality of your tendon tissue.*

The Healing Changes That Need To Take Place

Improve the quality of the tendon tissue. Hmm. What exactly does that mean? Well, recall from previous chapters...

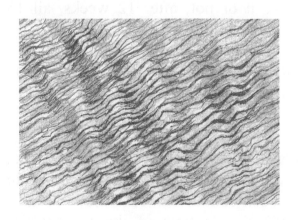

This is what your Achilles tendon tissue looks like now.

This is what your Achilles tendon tissue *needs* to look like.

The goal, then, is to get from the picture on the left to the picture on the right. But how? Well, by *reversing* the disorganized changes that have taken place. If we can somehow "jump start" things, and make these changes begin to happen, well, it'll be just a matter of time before your Achilles tendon heals up *and* you're back in action. But is there one single treatment that can pull all of this off? Absolutely! It's called *eccentric exercise*…

It Works!

So what exactly is eccentric exercise? Well, it's a type of strengthening exercise – but it's not done in the usual manner. When you exercise eccentrically, you don't lift weight, you *lower* it.

If this sounds funny to you, you're not alone. Despite its lack of popular use, this particular strengthening technique has been well studied and been around for awhile. One of the first studies done on eccentric exercise and the Achilles tendon took 15 patients subjects with pain in the mid-portion of their Achilles (Alfredson 1998).

All patients had tried the usual treatments (such as rest, anti-inflammatory medications, shoe inserts, etc) and unfortunately, all patients were also on a waiting list for surgery. Luckily though, a group of researchers had these patients perform daily eccentric exercises, and believe it or not, after 12 weeks, all 15 patients were satisfied and back doing their normal activities!

A few years later, another study treated 78 patients (having a total of 101 painful Achilles tendons) with eccentric exercise (Fahlstrom 2003). After 12 weeks, these researchers got satisfactory results in 90 out of the 101 tendons.

As the word got out, larger, better designed studies followed. For instance, many *randomized controlled trials*, which offer the highest form of proof in medicine that a treatment really works, have been conducted. And they too have shown eccentric exercise to be extremely effective in treating chronic Achilles tendinosis (Jonge 2010, Peterson 2007, Rompe 2007, and Roos 2004).

What's equally fascinating, is the research that's been done on the effects that eccentric exercise has on the actual structure of the Achilles tendon. Remember that two major changes researchers find in people with Achilles tendinosis are *wavy, disorganized tendon fibers* and *an abnormal increase in blood vessels (neovascularization)*. Well, it appears as though eccentric exercise can help fix those problems...

- this study looked at 25 patients that suffered from long-term, painful Achilles tendinosis (Ohberg 2004)

- all subjects has an ultrasound done on their Achilles tendon which showed tendon thickening and irregular tendon fiber structure

- researchers then had patients undergo eccentric exercise

- after 12 weeks of eccentric exercise, the follow-up ultrasound showed that the Achilles tendon thickness had decreased, and the tendon structure had normalized in most patients

- in another study by the same researcher, 41 tendons in 30 patients suffering from chronic Achilles tendinosis were examined by ultrasound (Ohberg 2004)

- ultrasound pictures showed an abnormal increase in the number of blood vessels in the tendon

- subjects then underwent 12 weeks of eccentric training

- 36 out of the 41 tendons became non-painful after the eccentric training

- in 32 of the 36 now non-painful tendons, ultrasound pictures showed no neovascularization

The Exercise

As you've just read, there's a lot of research showing that eccentric training can not only decrease pain, but also normalize the structure of your Achilles tendon. Use the following technique if you have Achilles tendinitis in just one leg – if you have tendinitis on both sides, use the alternate technique on page 67. So without any further delay, here's how the eccentric exercise goes that's been used in the studies you've just been reading about…

- find a step

- get into the above position

- the front half of your feet should be on the step,
  and your heels should be hanging freely

Step 1

- get into the above position, heels up high

- **do this by using your non-painful leg only**

- in other words, only the non-painful leg raises you up and does all the work. The painful leg should *not* help out.

- it is okay to hold on lightly to something to steady yourself if you need to

Step 2

- now raise your non-painful leg up so
  you're standing only on your painful leg

Step 3

- now all you do is lower the heel of your painful leg while keeping the knee straight

- try and lower your heel *below* the level of the step

- you've just done one repetition of the eccentric exercise!

- immediately after lowering your heel, get back in the starting position in Step 1 to do another repetition

- **and make sure you use your non-painful leg to to raise yourself back up into the starting position**

A few notes. It's really important that you use your *non-painful* leg to raise yourself *up* when doing the exercise – that's because we want the painful leg to do only one thing - lower its heel *below* the level of the step. And it's this lowering of the heel that is the "eccentric" exercise that causes your Achilles tendon to heal itself.

So how many times do you have to do it? Well, according to studies, you need to do 3 sets of 15 repetitions, twice a day. This means you'll be lowering the heel of your painful leg 15 times, resting a minute or two, lowering it 15 mores times, resting a minute or two, and then lowering it 15 more times. That makes 3 sets of 15 repetitions. And you need to do this 3 sets of 15 *twice* a day - once in the morning and once in the evening, seven days a week, for 12 weeks.

While this may sound like a lot, it really won't take as much time as you might think. As you'll see, it will probably take about ten minutes of your time in the morning, and 10 minutes of your time in the evening. And the good part about this eccentric exercise, is that all you'll need to do it is a step – so you can even do it at your workplace if you have some stairs there.

One more thing. If this exercise looks like it could be a bit uncomfortable, well, it might be. However this is one of the few times as a physical therapist that I actually tell patients to go ahead and do the exercise *even* if they experience discomfort.

Why? Because in the studies you've been reading about in this chapter, researchers have had their subjects *purposely* work thorough any discomfort they might encounter while doing the eccentric exercises – and are able to objectively show that doing it in this manner improved patients pain and normalized their tendon structure.

Therefore, I want you to start out doing the exercise using your own bodyweight, and when you can do the 3 sets of 15 repetitions, twice a day without any minor pain or discomfort, then you then need to *increase* the load on your Achilles tendon by adding more weight – as they also do in studies.

So just how do you add more weight? Well, the simplest way is to just put on a backpack that has a heavy book or two in it. When you do this, the exercise will probably become uncomfortable again, which is acceptable. As you can tell, the idea with the eccentric training is that it is okay to have some discomfort when you do the exercise, *but when you can do the exercise without any discomfort, add some weight to keep stimulating the healing process*. Keep repeating this as you need to over the 12 weeks.

And why 12 weeks? Well, remember that every time you do the exercise, you're sending a signal to your Achilles tendon to re-modeling itself. Recall the studies we discussed earlier in this chapter that show it takes a 12-week period for the Achilles tendon fibers to realign themselves and get rid of the abnormal neovascularization that has taken place.

While it may seem just plain nuts that you have to do a briefly uncomfortable exercise to get rid of pain, it's been shown *over and over* that doing eccentric exercise in this manner is highly effective, a few examples being the **five** randomized controlled trials listed at the bottom of page 30.

So do expect to have some discomfort while doing the exercise, *although you definitely need to stop if the pain becomes too intense*. You will also likely have some soreness in your leg muscles too, the gastrocnemius and soleus, but don't worry, that's completely normal and that typically goes away after a week or two after the muscles have gotten used to the exercise. Hang in there – this stuff really works!

12-Week Eccentric Exercise Log

All the knowledge in this book is virtually *useless* unless you put in into action. So, in order to help with this, I am including a daily exercise log, which you'll find on the following pages. It is a very useful tool to help readers stick with their eccentric exercise and is easy to use – just check off a box when you complete one set of 15 heel drops. Think of it as a 12-week countdown to a new Achilles tendon!

Week #1

Monday

AM Session		PM Session	
15 reps	☐	15 reps	☐
15 reps	☐	15 reps	☐
15 reps	☐	15 reps	☐

Tuesday

AM Session		PM Session	
15 reps	☐	15 reps	☐
15 reps	☐	15 reps	☐
15 reps	☐	15 reps	☐

Wednesday

AM Session		PM Session	
15 reps	☐	15 reps	☐
15 reps	☐	15 reps	☐
15 reps	☐	15 reps	☐

Thursday

AM Session		PM Session	
15 reps	☐	15 reps	☐
15 reps	☐	15 reps	☐
15 reps	☐	15 reps	☐

Friday

AM Session		PM Session	
15 reps	☐	15 reps	☐
15 reps	☐	15 reps	☐
15 reps	☐	15 reps	☐

Saturday

AM Session		PM Session	
15 reps	☐	15 reps	☐
15 reps	☐	15 reps	☐
15 reps	☐	15 reps	☐

Sunday

AM Session		PM Session	
15 reps	☐	15 reps	☐
15 reps	☐	15 reps	☐
15 reps	☐	15 reps	☐

Week #2

Monday

AM Session	PM Session
15 reps ☐	15 reps ☐
15 reps ☐	15 reps ☐
15 reps ☐	15 reps ☐

Tuesday

AM Session	PM Session
15 reps ☐	15 reps ☐
15 reps ☐	15 reps ☐
15 reps ☐	15 reps ☐

Wednesday

AM Session	PM Session
15 reps ☐	15 reps ☐
15 reps ☐	15 reps ☐
15 reps ☐	15 reps ☐

Thursday

AM Session	PM Session
15 reps ☐	15 reps ☐
15 reps ☐	15 reps ☐
15 reps ☐	15 reps ☐

Friday

AM Session	PM Session
15 reps ☐	15 reps ☐
15 reps ☐	15 reps ☐
15 reps ☐	15 reps ☐

Saturday

AM Session	PM Session
15 reps ☐	15 reps ☐
15 reps ☐	15 reps ☐
15 reps ☐	15 reps ☐

Sunday

AM Session	PM Session
15 reps ☐	15 reps ☐
15 reps ☐	15 reps ☐
15 reps ☐	15 reps ☐

Week #3

Monday

AM Session		PM Session	
15 reps	☐	15 reps	☐
15 reps	☐	15 reps	☐
15 reps	☐	15 reps	☐

Tuesday

AM Session		PM Session	
15 reps	☐	15 reps	☐
15 reps	☐	15 reps	☐
15 reps	☐	15 reps	☐

Wednesday

AM Session		PM Session	
15 reps	☐	15 reps	☐
15 reps	☐	15 reps	☐
15 reps	☐	15 reps	☐

Thursday

AM Session		PM Session	
15 reps	☐	15 reps	☐
15 reps	☐	15 reps	☐
15 reps	☐	15 reps	☐

Friday

AM Session		PM Session	
15 reps	☐	15 reps	☐
15 reps	☐	15 reps	☐
15 reps	☐	15 reps	☐

Saturday

AM Session		PM Session	
15 reps	☐	15 reps	☐
15 reps	☐	15 reps	☐
15 reps	☐	15 reps	☐

Sunday

AM Session		PM Session	
15 reps	☐	15 reps	☐
15 reps	☐	15 reps	☐
15 reps	☐	15 reps	☐

Week #4

Monday

AM Session		PM Session	
15 reps	☐	15 reps	☐
15 reps	☐	15 reps	☐
15 reps	☐	15 reps	☐

Tuesday

AM Session		PM Session	
15 reps	☐	15 reps	☐
15 reps	☐	15 reps	☐
15 reps	☐	15 reps	☐

Wednesday

AM Session		PM Session	
15 reps	☐	15 reps	☐
15 reps	☐	15 reps	☐
15 reps	☐	15 reps	☐

Thursday

AM Session		PM Session	
15 reps	☐	15 reps	☐
15 reps	☐	15 reps	☐
15 reps	☐	15 reps	☐

Friday

AM Session		PM Session	
15 reps	☐	15 reps	☐
15 reps	☐	15 reps	☐
15 reps	☐	15 reps	☐

Saturday

AM Session		PM Session	
15 reps	☐	15 reps	☐
15 reps	☐	15 reps	☐
15 reps	☐	15 reps	☐

Sunday

AM Session		PM Session	
15 reps	☐	15 reps	☐
15 reps	☐	15 reps	☐
15 reps	☐	15 reps	☐

Week #5

Monday

AM Session		PM Session	
15 reps	☐	15 reps	☐
15 reps	☐	15 reps	☐
15 reps	☐	15 reps	☐

Tuesday

AM Session		PM Session	
15 reps	☐	15 reps	☐
15 reps	☐	15 reps	☐
15 reps	☐	15 reps	☐

Wednesday

AM Session		PM Session	
15 reps	☐	15 reps	☐
15 reps	☐	15 reps	☐
15 reps	☐	15 reps	☐

Thursday

AM Session		PM Session	
15 reps	☐	15 reps	☐
15 reps	☐	15 reps	☐
15 reps	☐	15 reps	☐

Friday

AM Session		PM Session	
15 reps	☐	15 reps	☐
15 reps	☐	15 reps	☐
15 reps	☐	15 reps	☐

Saturday

AM Session		PM Session	
15 reps	☐	15 reps	☐
15 reps	☐	15 reps	☐
15 reps	☐	15 reps	☐

Sunday

AM Session		PM Session	
15 reps	☐	15 reps	☐
15 reps	☐	15 reps	☐
15 reps	☐	15 reps	☐

Week #6

Monday

AM Session		PM Session	
15 reps	☐	15 reps	☐
15 reps	☐	15 reps	☐
15 reps	☐	15 reps	☐

Tuesday

AM Session		PM Session	
15 reps	☐	15 reps	☐
15 reps	☐	15 reps	☐
15 reps	☐	15 reps	☐

Wednesday

AM Session		PM Session	
15 reps	☐	15 reps	☐
15 reps	☐	15 reps	☐
15 reps	☐	15 reps	☐

Thursday

AM Session		PM Session	
15 reps	☐	15 reps	☐
15 reps	☐	15 reps	☐
15 reps	☐	15 reps	☐

Friday

AM Session		PM Session	
15 reps	☐	15 reps	☐
15 reps	☐	15 reps	☐
15 reps	☐	15 reps	☐

Saturday

AM Session		PM Session	
15 reps	☐	15 reps	☐
15 reps	☐	15 reps	☐
15 reps	☐	15 reps	☐

Sunday

AM Session		PM Session	
15 reps	☐	15 reps	☐
15 reps	☐	15 reps	☐
15 reps	☐	15 reps	☐

Week #7

Monday

AM Session		PM Session	
15 reps	☐	15 reps	☐
15 reps	☐	15 reps	☐
15 reps	☐	15 reps	☐

Tuesday

AM Session		PM Session	
15 reps	☐	15 reps	☐
15 reps	☐	15 reps	☐
15 reps	☐	15 reps	☐

Wednesday

AM Session		PM Session	
15 reps	☐	15 reps	☐
15 reps	☐	15 reps	☐
15 reps	☐	15 reps	☐

Thursday

AM Session		PM Session	
15 reps	☐	15 reps	☐
15 reps	☐	15 reps	☐
15 reps	☐	15 reps	☐

Friday

AM Session		PM Session	
15 reps	☐	15 reps	☐
15 reps	☐	15 reps	☐
15 reps	☐	15 reps	☐

Saturday

AM Session		PM Session	
15 reps	☐	15 reps	☐
15 reps	☐	15 reps	☐
15 reps	☐	15 reps	☐

Sunday

AM Session		PM Session	
15 reps	☐	15 reps	☐
15 reps	☐	15 reps	☐
15 reps	☐	15 reps	☐

Week #8

Monday

AM Session	PM Session
15 reps ☐	15 reps ☐
15 reps ☐	15 reps ☐
15 reps ☐	15 reps ☐

Tuesday

AM Session	PM Session
15 reps ☐	15 reps ☐
15 reps ☐	15 reps ☐
15 reps ☐	15 reps ☐

Wednesday

AM Session	PM Session
15 reps ☐	15 reps ☐
15 reps ☐	15 reps ☐
15 reps ☐	15 reps ☐

Thursday

AM Session	PM Session
15 reps ☐	15 reps ☐
15 reps ☐	15 reps ☐
15 reps ☐	15 reps ☐

Friday

AM Session	PM Session
15 reps ☐	15 reps ☐
15 reps ☐	15 reps ☐
15 reps ☐	15 reps ☐

Saturday

AM Session	PM Session
15 reps ☐	15 reps ☐
15 reps ☐	15 reps ☐
15 reps ☐	15 reps ☐

Sunday

AM Session	PM Session
15 reps ☐	15 reps ☐
15 reps ☐	15 reps ☐
15 reps ☐	15 reps ☐

Week #9

Monday

AM Session		PM Session	
15 reps	☐	15 reps	☐
15 reps	☐	15 reps	☐
15 reps	☐	15 reps	☐

Tuesday

AM Session		PM Session	
15 reps	☐	15 reps	☐
15 reps	☐	15 reps	☐
15 reps	☐	15 reps	☐

Wednesday

AM Session		PM Session	
15 reps	☐	15 reps	☐
15 reps	☐	15 reps	☐
15 reps	☐	15 reps	☐

Thursday

AM Session		PM Session	
15 reps	☐	15 reps	☐
15 reps	☐	15 reps	☐
15 reps	☐	15 reps	☐

Friday

AM Session		PM Session	
15 reps	☐	15 reps	☐
15 reps	☐	15 reps	☐
15 reps	☐	15 reps	☐

Saturday

AM Session		PM Session	
15 reps	☐	15 reps	☐
15 reps	☐	15 reps	☐
15 reps	☐	15 reps	☐

Sunday

AM Session		PM Session	
15 reps	☐	15 reps	☐
15 reps	☐	15 reps	☐
15 reps	☐	15 reps	☐

Week #10

Monday

AM Session		PM Session	
15 reps	☐	15 reps	☐
15 reps	☐	15 reps	☐
15 reps	☐	15 reps	☐

Tuesday

AM Session		PM Session	
15 reps	☐	15 reps	☐
15 reps	☐	15 reps	☐
15 reps	☐	15 reps	☐

Wednesday

AM Session		PM Session	
15 reps	☐	15 reps	☐
15 reps	☐	15 reps	☐
15 reps	☐	15 reps	☐

Thursday

AM Session		PM Session	
15 reps	☐	15 reps	☐
15 reps	☐	15 reps	☐
15 reps	☐	15 reps	☐

Friday

AM Session		PM Session	
15 reps	☐	15 reps	☐
15 reps	☐	15 reps	☐
15 reps	☐	15 reps	☐

Saturday

AM Session		PM Session	
15 reps	☐	15 reps	☐
15 reps	☐	15 reps	☐
15 reps	☐	15 reps	☐

Sunday

AM Session		PM Session	
15 reps	☐	15 reps	☐
15 reps	☐	15 reps	☐
15 reps	☐	15 reps	☐

Week #11

Monday

AM Session	PM Session
15 reps ☐	15 reps ☐
15 reps ☐	15 reps ☐
15 reps ☐	15 reps ☐

Tuesday

AM Session	PM Session
15 reps ☐	15 reps ☐
15 reps ☐	15 reps ☐
15 reps ☐	15 reps ☐

Wednesday

AM Session	PM Session
15 reps ☐	15 reps ☐
15 reps ☐	15 reps ☐
15 reps ☐	15 reps ☐

Thursday

AM Session	PM Session
15 reps ☐	15 reps ☐
15 reps ☐	15 reps ☐
15 reps ☐	15 reps ☐

Friday

AM Session	PM Session
15 reps ☐	15 reps ☐
15 reps ☐	15 reps ☐
15 reps ☐	15 reps ☐

Saturday

AM Session	PM Session
15 reps ☐	15 reps ☐
15 reps ☐	15 reps ☐
15 reps ☐	15 reps ☐

Sunday

AM Session	PM Session
15 reps ☐	15 reps ☐
15 reps ☐	15 reps ☐
15 reps ☐	15 reps ☐

Week #12

Monday

AM Session	PM Session
15 reps ☐	15 reps ☐
15 reps ☐	15 reps ☐
15 reps ☐	15 reps ☐

Tuesday

AM Session	PM Session
15 reps ☐	15 reps ☐
15 reps ☐	15 reps ☐
15 reps ☐	15 reps ☐

Wednesday

AM Session	PM Session
15 reps ☐	15 reps ☐
15 reps ☐	15 reps ☐
15 reps ☐	15 reps ☐

Thursday

AM Session	PM Session
15 reps ☐	15 reps ☐
15 reps ☐	15 reps ☐
15 reps ☐	15 reps ☐

Friday

AM Session	PM Session
15 reps ☐	15 reps ☐
15 reps ☐	15 reps ☐
15 reps ☐	15 reps ☐

Saturday

AM Session	PM Session
15 reps ☐	15 reps ☐
15 reps ☐	15 reps ☐
15 reps ☐	15 reps ☐

Sunday

AM Session	PM Session
15 reps ☐	15 reps ☐
15 reps ☐	15 reps ☐
15 reps ☐	15 reps ☐

Key Points

✓ **Achilles tendinosis is a problem of failed tendon healing**

✓ **eccentric exercise will not only decrease pain, but also helps the tendon heal by causing the Achilles tendon to structurally re-model itself back to normal. For instance, it has been documented that tendon fibers are back to their normal alignment, and neovascularization disappears after 12 weeks of eccentric exercise.**

✓ **there are many randomized controlled trials that have successfully treated Achilles tendon pain using eccentric exercise that may be briefly uncomfortable to do. However, you should stop if the pain becomes too intense.**

✓ **it is recommended that you do 3 sets of 15 repetitions of the eccentric exercise, twice a day for 12 weeks**

✓ **when you can do 3 sets of 15 repetitions, twice a day without any minor pain or discomfort, you then need to *increase* the load on your Achilles tendon by adding more weight. Using a backpack with some books or weights in it is the easiest way to do this.**

✓ **having muscle soreness from doing eccentric exercise is normal and usually goes away after a week or two after the muscles get used to the exercise**

How Much Activity Is Safe To Do While You're Recovering

As we've mentioned throughout this book, most people with a painful Achilles tendon suffer from a condition called *tendinosis*, which is caused by overuse. So the question now is, as you're doing your eccentric exercises, and waiting for your Achilles tendon to structurally re-model its fibers, how much exercise and activity is safe to do? For example, is it okay to run or bike a little?

Well, that's a really good question, as you wouldn't want to keep overusing your Achilles tendon when it's trying to heal. Remember that the Achilles tendon gets pulled on every time as you plantarflex or push out your foot, which goes on all day long as the circles in the following pictures show…

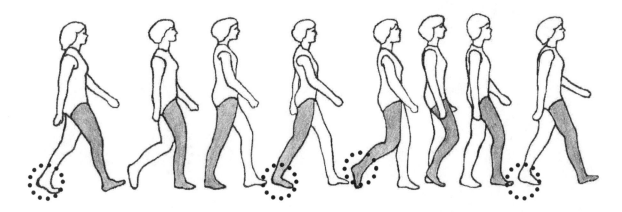

Figure 24. Walking

Figure 25. Running

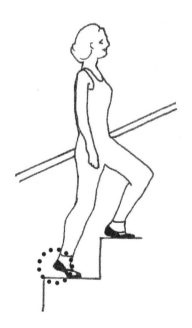

Figure 26. Climbing stairs.

Figure 27. Coming up on your toes.

As we see, that the Achilles tendon sure gets a lot of use! What's more, many readers probably participate in a sport too. So, how much activity is safe to do, if any?

Well, a very well done study, recently published in the *American Journal of Sports Medicine* has shed a lot of light on this. While the thinking for years used to be to give your Achilles tendon a period of total rest, we now know that might not be the best thing to do…

- 38 patients with painful Achilles tendons were randomized into one of two groups (Silbernagel 2007)

- the first group did exercises for their Achilles tendons, which included eccentric exercises, for at least 12 weeks. Additionally, they were **not** allowed to do any activities that aggravated their pain, such as running or jumping, for the first 6 weeks of the study.

- the second group did the exact same exercises as group one, *except they were allowed to do whatever activities they wanted to, as long as their pain didn't get above a "5" on a zero to ten pain scale*

- at the end of the study, both groups improved significantly, and at the same rate. Interestingly, no negative effects occurred in group two that was allowed to continue tendon loading activities.

Based on the results of this randomized controlled trial, it would appear that it is actually okay to continue doing activities that stress your Achilles tendon – as long as the activities don't cause the pain to go above a "5". So the next question is, how much pain is a "5"?

Well, the scale goes from the number 0, all the way to number 10. And if you were having no pain at all in your Achilles tendon while doing an activity (like running), you would rate your pain a "0". On the other hand, if you're having the worst pain imaginable in your Achilles tendon while you're doing an activity, you would rate your pain a "10". Therefore, a rating of "5" is in the middle of these two pain levels.

Key Points

✓ although briefly uncomfortable eccentric exercise has been proven to decrease pain and re-model the Achilles tendon back to normal, it is not good to overstress the Achilles for extended periods as it is trying to heal

✓ however, it is not necessary to completely rest it either

✓ as you are doing your eccentric exercises, which stimulate your Achilles to heal over a 12-week period, it is okay to continue with things such as sport activities, as long as your pain level doesn't go above a "5" on a 0 to 10 scale

---

6 Measure Your Progress

Okay. You've learned all about the Achilles tendon, tendinosis, started the eccentric exercise, and are on the road to recovery. So now what should you expect?

Well, we all know you should expect to get better. But what exactly does *better* mean? As a physical therapist treating patients, it means two distinct things to me:

- your Achilles tendon starts to *feel* better

and

- your Achilles tendon starts to *work* better

And so, when a patient returns for a follow-up visit, I re-assess them, looking for specific changes in their Achilles tendon pain, as well as their Achilles tendon function.

In this book, I'm going to recommend that readers do the same thing periodically. Why? Simply because people in pain can't always see the progress they're making. For instance sometimes a person's pain is exactly the same, but they aren't aware that they can now actually do some motions or tasks that they couldn't do before – a sure sign that things are healing. *Or*, sometimes a person still has significant pain but they're not aware that it's actually occurring less frequently – yet another good indication that positive changes are taking place.

Whatever the case may be, if a person isn't looking at the bigger picture, and doesn't *think* they're getting any better, they're likely to get discouraged and stop doing the exercises altogether – even though they really might have been on the right track!

On the other hand though, what if you periodically check your progress and are keenly aware that your Achilles tendon has made some changes for the better? What if you can *positively* see objective results? My guess is that you're going to be giving yourself a healthy dose of motivation to finish the 12-week program.

Having said that, I'm going to show you exactly what to check for from time to time so that you can monitor *all* the changes that are taking place in your Achilles tendon. I call them "outcomes" and there are two of them.

Outcome #1:
Look for Changes in Your Pain

First of all, you should look for changes in your pain. I know this may sound silly, but sometimes it's my job to get a person to see that their pain *is* actually improving. You see, a lot of people come to physical therapy thinking they're going to be pain-free right away. Then, when they're not instantly better and still having pain, they often start to worry and become discouraged. Truth is, I have seen very few people start an exercise program and get instantly better. Better yes, but not *instantly* better.

Over the years, I have found that patients usually respond to therapy in a quite predictable pattern. When doing an unfamiliar exercise, most patients will experience a period for a week or two where they have increased soreness. This is normal and occurs because your joints, muscles and tendons just aren't used to an exercise yet. However after this "break in" period, one of three things will almost always occur as your Achilles tendon begins to turn the corner and get better:

- your Achilles tendon pain is just as intense as always, however now it is occurring much less frequently

or

- your Achilles tendon pain is now *less* intense, even though it still occurring just as frequently

or

- you start to notice less intense Achilles tendon pain *and* it is now occurring less frequently

The point here is to make sure that you keep a sharp eye out for these three scenarios as you continue along with the eccentric exercises for the 12-week period. If *any* of them occur, it will be a sure sign that the program is working. You can then look forward to the pain gradually getting better, usually over the weeks to come.

Outcome #2:
Look for Changes in Achilles Tendon Function

Looking at how well your Achilles tendon is working is very important because sometimes Achilles tendon function improves *before* the pain does. For example, sometimes a patient will do the exercises for a while, and although their Achilles still hurts, they are able to do many activities that they haven't been able to in a while – a really good indicator that healing is taking place *and* that the pain should be easing up soon.

While measuring your Achilles tendon function may sound like a pain in the butt, it doesn't have to be. One option that readers can use is a quick and easy assessment tool known as the *Victorian Institute of Sport Assessment – Achilles* questionnaire, or VISA-A for short.

Developed by the Victorian Institute of Sport tendon study group (Robinson 2001), the VISA-A has actually been around for awhile and was specially made to document the stiffness, pain, and function in people with Achilles tendon problems. It is very well researched and has been shown to be:

- *valid*, meaning that it actually measures what it's supposed to be measuring (Robinson 2001)

- *reliable*, meaning that you can get the same result with repeated testing (Robinson 2001)

- *responsive*, meaning that it has the ability to detect changes in a person over time (Silbernagel 2007)

Additionally, the VISA-A takes about 5 minutes to complete and can be scored with a simple calculator in under a minute. Now that's my kinda test!

So what exactly does the VISA-A involve? Not much. The questionnaire consists of eight questions, *so you simply read each one and put a check in the box that best applies to your particular situation.* After that, just go back and add up the numbers that are by the boxes you've checked to get your total score.

And what does the score mean? Well, if you score 100, that would be a perfect score – and that's what a person with *no* Achilles tendon symptoms would have. On the other hand, the lower the score, the worse off you're doing. On the next few pages is a copy of the VISA-A.

The VISA-A Questionnaire

IN THIS QUESTIONNAIRE, THE TERM PAIN REFERS SPECIFICALLY TO PAIN IN THE ACHILLES TENDON REGION

1. For how many minutes do you have stiffness in the Achilles region on first getting up?

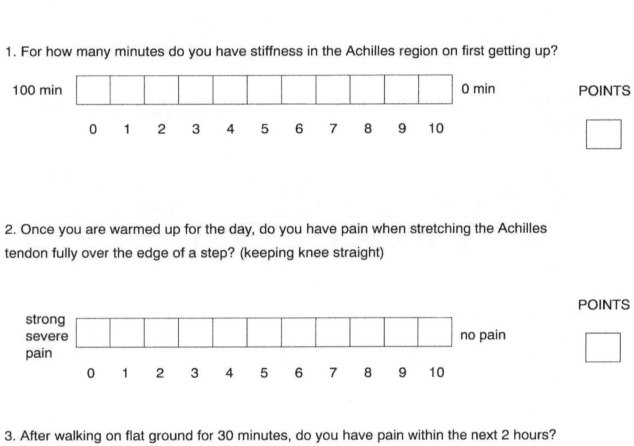

100 min   0 min   POINTS

        0   1   2   3   4   5   6   7   8   9   10

2. Once you are warmed up for the day, do you have pain when stretching the Achilles tendon fully over the edge of a step? (keeping knee straight)

POINTS

strong
severe   no pain
pain

        0   1   2   3   4   5   6   7   8   9   10

3. After walking on flat ground for 30 minutes, do you have pain within the next 2 hours? (If unable to walk on flat ground for 30 minutes because of pain, score 0 for this question).

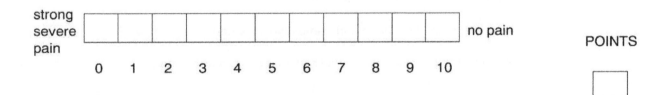

strong
severe   no pain
pain   POINTS

        0   1   2   3   4   5   6   7   8   9   10

4. Do you have pain walking downstairs with normal gait cycle?

| strong severe pain | | | | | | | | | | | | no pain |

0   1   2   3   4   5   6   7   8   9   10

POINTS

5. Do you have pain during or immediately after doing 10 (single leg) heel raises from a flat surface?

| strong severe pain | | | | | | | | | | | | no pain |

0   1   2   3   4   5   6   7   8   9   10

POINTS

6. How many single leg hops can you do without pain?

| 0 | | | | | | | | | | | | 10 |

0   1   2   3   4   5   6   7   8   9   10

POINTS

7. Are you currently undertaking sport or other physical activity?

0 ☐ Not at all

4 ☐ Modified training ± modified competition

7 ☐ Full training ± competition but not at same level as when symptoms began

10 ☐ Competing at the same or higher level as when symptoms began

POINTS

8. Please complete **EITHER A, B or C** in this question.

- If you have **no pain while undertaking Achilles tendon loading sports** please complete **Q8A only**.
- If you have **pain while undertaking Achilles tendon loading sports but it does not stop you from completing the activity**, please complete **Q8B only**.
- If you have **pain that stops you from completing Achilles tendon loading sports**, please complete **Q8C only**.

A. If you have **no pain** while undertaking **Achilles tendon loading sports**, for how long can you train/practise?

POINTS

NIL	1–10 mins	11–20 mins	21–30 mins	>30 mins
☐	☐	☐	☐	☐
0	7	14	21	30

OR

B. If you have some pain while undertaking **Achilles tendon loading sports**, but it does not stop you from completing your training/practice, for how long can you train/practise?

POINTS

NIL	1–10 mins	11–20 mins	21–30 mins	>30 mins
☐	☐	☐	☐	☐
0	4	10	14	20

OR

C. If you have **pain that stops you** from completing your training/practice in **Achilles tendon loading sports**, for how long can you train/practise?

POINTS

NIL	1–10 mins	11–20 mins	21–30 mins	>30 mins
☐	☐	☐	☐	☐
0	2	5	7	10

TOTAL SCORE (/100) ☐ %

So how'd you do? Remember, the lower the number, the worse off you are, and if you scored pretty low, well, that's okay – it gives us a starting point to judge how much you're progressing over time. Just re-take the VISA-A every few weeks or so, and as you continue with the eccentric exercises, you should see your score go higher and higher as time passes.

Key Points

✓ being aware of your progress is an important part of treating Achilles tendon pain – it motivates you to keep doing the exercises

✓ look for the pain to become less *intense*, less *frequent*, or both to let you know that the exercises are helping

✓ sometimes your Achilles tendon starts to work better *before* it starts to feel better. Taking the VISA-A from time to time makes you aware of these improvements.

Comprehensive List of Supporting References

It's true! All the information in this book is based on randomized controlled trials and scientific studies that have been published in peer-reviewed journals. Since I know there are readers out there that like to actually check out the information for themselves, I've included the references for every study I have cited in this book...

Chapter 1

Astrom M, et al. Chronic achilles tendinopathy. A survey of surgical and histopathologic findings. *Clinical Orthopaedics and Related Research* 1995;316:151-164.

Astrom M, et al. Imaging in chronic achilles tendinopathy: a comparison of ultrasonography, magnetic resonance imaging and surgical findings in 27 histologically verified cases. *Skeletal Radiol* 1996;25:615-620.

Simmonds FA. The diagnosis of the ruptured achilles tendon. *Practitioner* 1957;179:56-58.

Chapter 2

Chen T, et al. The arterial anatomy of the achilles tendon: anatomical study and clinical implications. *Clinical Anatomy* 2009;22:377-385.

Movin T, et al. Tendon pathology in long-standing achillodynia. Biopsy findings in 40 patients. *Acta Orthop Scand* 1997;68:170-175.

Movin T, et al. Intratendinous alterations as imaged by ultrasound and contrast medium-enhanced magnetic resonance in chronic achillodynia. *Foot and Ankle Intternational* 1998;19:311-317.

Rolf C, et al. Etiology, histopathology, and outcome in achillodynia. *Foot and Ankle International* 1997;18:565-569.

Shalabi A, et al. Dynamic contrast-enhanced MR imaging and histopathology in chronic achilles tendinosis. A longitudinal study of 15 patients. *Acta Radiologica* 2002;43:198-206.

Stein V, et al. Quantitative assessment of intravascular volume of the human achilles tendon. *Acta Orthop Scand* 2000;71:60-63.

Szaro P, et al Fascicles of the adult human achilles tendon – an anatomical study. *Ann Anat* 2009;191:586-593.

Zantop T, et al. Quantitative assessment of blood vessels of the human achilles tendon: an immunohistochemical cadaver study. *Arch Orthop Trauma Surg* 2003;123:501-504.

Chapter 3

Rompe J, et al. Eccentric loading, shock-wave treatment, or a wait-and-see policy for tendinopathy of the main body of tendo achillis. *The American Journal of Sports Medicine* 2007;35:374-383.

Chapter 4

Alfredson H, et al. Heavy-load eccentric calf muscle training for the treatment of chronic achilles tendinosis. *The American Journal of Sports Medicine* 1998;26:360-366.

De Jonge S, et al. One-year follow-up of a randomized controlled trial of added splinting to eccentric exercises in chronic midportion achilles tendinopathy. *Br J Sports Med 2010*;44:673-677.

Fahlstrom M, et al. Chronic achilles tendon pain treated with eccentric calf-muscle training. *Knee Surg Sports Traumatol Arthrosc* 2003;11:327-333.

Ohberg L, et al. Eccentric training in patients with chronic achilles tendinosis: normalised tendon structure and decreased thickness at follow up. *Br J Sports Med* 2004;38:8-11.

Ohberg L, et al. Effects on neovascularization behind the good results with eccentric training in chronic mid-portion achilles tendinosis? *Knee Surg Sports Traumatol Arthrosc* 2004;12:465-470.

Peterson W, et al. Chronic achilles tendinopathy. A prospective randomized study comparing the therapeutic effect of eccentric training, the airheel brace, and a combination of both. *The American Journal of Sports Medicine* 2007;35:1659-1667.

Rompe J, et al. Eccentric loading, shock-wave treatment, or a wait-and-see policy for tendinopathy of the main body of tendo achillis. *The American Journal of Sports Medicine* 2007;35:374-383.

Roos E, et al. Clinical improvement after 6 weeks of eccentric exercise in patients with mid-portion achilles tendinopathy – a randomized trial with 1-year follow-up. *Scand J Med Sci Sports* 2004;14:286-295.

Chapter 5

Silbernagel K, et al. Continued sports activity, using a pain-monitoring model, during rehabilitation in patients with achilles tendinopathy. A randomized controlled study. *The American Journal of Sports Medicine* 2007;35:897-906.

Chapter 6

Robinson JM, et al. The VISA-A questionnaire: a valid and reliable index of the clinical severity of achilles tendinopathy. *Br J Sports Med* 2001;35:335-341.

Silbernagel K, et al. Full symptomatic recovery does not insure full recovery of muscle tendon function in patients with achilles tendinopathy. *Br J Sports Med* 2007;41:276-280.

Alternate Technique for Treating Bilateral Achilles Tendinitis

If you have Achilles tendinitis in *both* tendons, you will be doing the same eccentric exercise discussed in Chapter 4, except the technique is a little different getting your foot into the raised heel position. It goes as follows…

- find a step

- get into the above position

- the front half of your feet should be on the step, and your heels should be hanging freely

Step 1

- We're going to exercise the right heel first, so begin by taking a step *up* to the next step with the left foot, making sure that you place your *whole* foot on the step.

- Now with your left foot planted, **you should be able to raise up the right heel by pushing up with the left leg - keeping most of your weight on your left foot.**

- In other words, only the left leg on the upper step does the work. The right leg should *not* help out getting the right heel into the raised position.

- It is recommended to hold on lightly to something to steady yourself.

Step 2

- next, take your left foot off the step so you're standing only on your right leg

- you should be in the above position with your right heel raised up high

Step 3

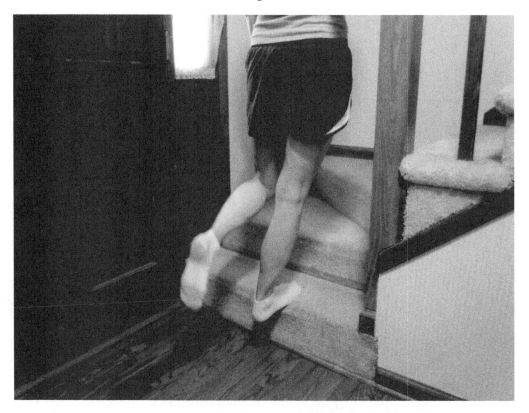

- now all you do is lower your right heel down to the floor while keeping the knee straight

- try and lower your heel *below* the level of the step

- you've just done one repetition of the eccentric exercise!

- immediately after lowering your right heel, go back to Step 1 and repeat this sequence to do another repetition

- **remember to use your left leg to raise yourself back up into the starting position**

- when you're finished with the right side, use the same technique for the left side (take a step up with the right leg to get the left heel into the raised position)

- it is recommended to do 3 sets of 15 reps for each side, twice a day (see page 36)

CPSIA information can be obtained at www.ICGtesting.com
Printed in the USA
BVOW11s1159070115

382303BV00010B/81/P